Carlos Montenegro

TOLEDO

BONECHI

*Some significant examples of local
handicraft production: pottery and swords.*

© Copyright 1994 by Casa Editrice Bonechi, via Cairoli 18/b - 50131 Florence - Italy
Tel. 55/576841 - Telex 571323 CEB - Fax 55/5000766
All rights reserved. No part of this book may be reproduced without the written permission of the Publisher.
Printed in Italy by Centro Stampa Editoriale Bonechi.
Photographs from the Archives of Casa Editrice Bonechi taken by Alessandro Saragosa.
Translated by Susan Fraser.

ISBN 88-7009-548-7

A BIT OF HISTORY

«El rio Tajo», or Tagus River, encircles the granitic rock on which Toledo stands. The four kilometres of the carretera de Circunvalación that connect the Puente de San Martín to the famous Puente de Alcántara provide the back-drop for a magnificent sight: the Gothic and Moorish walls that surround the city and house some of the most precious treasures of mudéjar art, that incredible mixture of Christian and Arabic influences.

The granite massif placed in the centre of the boundless Spanish plateau could not escape ancient Iberian tribes: the Carpathians built their first capital there and Toledo began its history as a city of destiny.

The Romans arrived in Toledo almost two centuries before the birth of Christ. In 192 B.C. the Roman army took the city by storm and made it the strategic centre of a colony. «Toletum», as Livy called it, became a fortified city, an essential link for the military defence of Roman expansionism.

Only four centuries later, during the III century A.D., the barbarians managed to burst into «Toletum»; the first new conquerors were the Alans followed in 418 by the Visigoths whose history was connected for three centuries to the initial splendours of the city.

In 579, the Visigoth king Leovigild I made Toledo the capital of his vast kingdom. His dynasty resisted until 709. Under the dominion of Reccared the Council of Toledo, the third in Christian history, was held in 589; apart from confirming the Visigoth king's conversion to Christianity, it unified Spain under a single religion.

Toledo was already established as one of the cultural and religious capitals of Spain. The oldest Spanish archdiocese was installed in Toledo and to date Catholic primacy of the city is nationally acknowledged.

The Visigoth reign could not curb the Arab invasion: Tarek defeated the Christian kings at the Battle of Guadalete in 711 and conquered Toledo. The city was rebaptized «Tolaitola» and lost its leading role in favour of the Caliphate of Cordova. During Muslim rule, the city flourished, even if signs of the intolerance against the Caliphs of Cordova were plainly visible. Several times the city rebelled and for forty years it managed to maintain its political independence. The Christian reconquest of Spain reached a turning point with the fall of Toledo: on the 25th May 1085 the army of Alfonso VI of Castile regained control of the city which then became the outpost of the interminable dissension between Christians and Muslims. Two years later, Toledo was already the capital of Castile, having dethroned Leon. Alfonso VIII bestowed on it the title of imperial city. Several times the Arabs tried to reconquer Toledo but not even with the sieges of 1197 and 1295 did they succeed. And the city, despite its state of continuous war, experienced one of its golden moments. Ferdinand III, the Saint (1217-1252), made it the powerful centre of a rich cultural life. It was he, together with the archbishop Rodrigo Ximénez de Rada, who laid the foundation stone of Toledo Cathedral. And it was his successor, Alfonso X, the Wise (1252-1284), who founded the School for Translators which made Toledo an authentic capital of Medieval culture. During this period the city became the meeting point for three great cultures: Christians, Muslims and Jews lived in harmony in Toledo. Also as far as the arts were concerned, the various influences blended in: even the synagogues felt the inevitable, splendid effects of the Moorish presence. There were years of great prosperity for Toledo.

Its decadence commenced with the victory of intolerance: between 1335 and 1391, real «pogroms» exploded against the rich Jewish community. At the end of the century the Christians did not hesitate to kill Jews during a service in the synagogue of Santa María la Blanca. Some decades later, the Inquisition burnt heretics at the stake and in 1492 the Jews were driven out of Spain.

In later years, Toledo was also the heart of the revolt of the «Comuneros», the movement that tried to defend civic freedom against the abuse of power of the Spanish sovereigns. The leader of the Comuneros, Juan de Padilla, was from Toledo. He fell during the Battle of Villalar and his place was taken by his wife María Pacheco. Only after her escape to Portugal did Toledo surrend. But Toledo paid a high price for this rebellion; in 1560 Philip II removed the title of imperial city from Toledo and made nearby Madrid the capital. Toledo kept its religious importance but never returned to past glories. It became part of Spanish history, sharing its vicissitudes. It was no longer the centre of the Spanish political scene but it kept intact the treasures of a small city unique in the world.

...e Alcazar and the Alcántara bridge.   _The north façade of the Alcazar._

ALCAZAR

The fact that this fortress is situated at the city's high-
...t point has been all-important for both its history and
...chitecture. Its privileged strategic position induced
...omans, Visigoths, Moors and Christians to gradually
...uild their fortresses on top of the ruins of the previous
...nes.

The city's Christian conqueror, Alfonso VI, ordered
...at the castle built by the Moors be restored. The cas-
...e, left in the hands of the legendary Commander Ro-
...rigo Diaz de Vivar — «El Cid Campeador» — was in
...ct severely damaged during the battle fought for do-
...inion of the city. During the XVIth century, Emperor
...harles V of Hapsburg had his monumental palace
...rected here. He commissioned the famous architect Al-
...onso de Covarrubias, who designed the main north-
...acing façade, to do the work. Francisco de Villapando
...nd Juan de Herrera contributed to its construction.
...he central patio and main staircase are attributed to

the former, whereas the latter designed the south-facing
façade.

At the beginning of the XVIIIth century, the castle
was once again destroyed by the English and Portuguese
troops who fought alongside the Archduke Charles of
Austria against Philip V of Anjou in the Wars of Succes-
sion for the Spanish throne.

In 1772, after restoration was carried out by Ventura
Rodriguez, the Alcazar was converted into a charity
institution called the «Real Casa de la Caridad» according to a decree emanated by Charles III and remained
under the direction of Cardinal Lorenzana. This home
housed as many as 700 persons, mainly beggars, who
were offered hospitality and work.

During the nineteenth century the Alcazar was once
again destroyed due to pressure exerted by Napoleon
Bonaparte's armed forces. The fire raged for three days
and three nights. It was then rebuilt between 1867 and

5

Another view of the Alcazar.

1882, when the building was converted into the Military Infantry Academy.

The last disaster dates back to the XXth century. When the Spanish Civil War broke out, the Commander of the «Escuela General Gimnasia de Toledo», José Moscardó Ituarte, prevented from directly joining the insurgents, assembled the troops supporting General Franco's uprising in the Alcázar, thus establishing a nationalistic nucleus in the rampart of Toledo. The Republican troops did not waste time taking a stand and prepared a siege that lasted 72 days, during which time almost the entire building was destroyed. Not only soldiers and officers were besieged, but also women and children. On that occasion, General Moscardó chose to sacrifice his son rather than surrender to the enemy. The besieged managed to hold the fort until General Varela's troops arrived. This episode is documented in detail in the halls of the present day Alcázar, which was rebuilt along the lines of the previous project. On leaving the Alcázar, one can admire a monument dedicated to the city's defenders during the siege attributed to Juan de Avalos.

The central courtyard of the
Alcazar with the monument
to Charles V (copy by L. Leoni).

Alcazar, bust of the
Commander José Moscardó Ituarte
and evidence of the Civil War.

Plaza de la Villa (or del Ayuntamiento) with the Town Hall and Archbishop's Palace.

The main façade of the Cathedral

LA PLAZA DEL AYUNTAMIENTO

Also known as Plaza de la Villa, it is flanked to the south by the Town Hall and Law Court, to the west by the Archbishop's Palace and to the east by the Cathedral. The first of these three buildings was designed by Jorge Manuel Theotocopouli, El Greco's son, at the beginning of the XVIIth century. Built in Renaissance style, it features two interesting twin towers covered with slate and crowned with spires.

The original nucleus of the Archbishop's Palace was the house of Archbishop Jiménez de Rada, built during the XIIIth century on land ceded by Alfonso VIII. It was then transformed and extended by other archbishops. The arch that joins it to the Cathedral at the height of

the Puerta de Mollete was erected by Cardinal Mendoza. It owes its present appearance to an initiative of Cardinal Lorenzana who had it demolished to give it it's present day structure. The outside façade in Neoclassic style was constructed during the XVIIIth century.

Even though the Law Court was built recently, its appearance has been adapted to successfully blend in with the square's architecture.

THE CATHEDRAL

Unlike the cathedrals in other Spanish cities such as Seville or Jaén, on which we have not only documents but also archaeological finds feeding us information as to their origins and subsequent transformations, we have no definite information on Toledo Cathedral; in

Cathedral, the Puerta del Perdón.

Cathedral, the Puerta del Reloj.

*Cathedral,
view of the Cloister*

fact, we only have indirect references in documents dating back to that period and very slight traces of how it was possibly built in the past. We do not know which buildings existed during Roman times, even if it is assumed that they were important basilicas, temples or civic buildings near to the city's «forum». There is a lack of information on the Visigothic and Moorish settlements. Legend has it that the first temple to be built on this site was that of S. Ildefonso, patron of the city, to whom the Virgin appeared, thus rewarding him for the fervent defence of his virginity. When the city was conquered by the Arabs, the temple was converted into a mosque; in 1085 it became Christian once again thanks to Alfonso VI. It was then destroyed and in its place construction was commenced on the present

building in 1227, at the time of Ferdinand III the Saint. The new basilica is today considered one of the finest examples of XIIIth century Gothic architecture, with evident references to the French model; however the Castilian influence can be noted in that more balanced proportions replace the predominance of the vertical rhythm.

The Cathedral consists of a nave and four aisles of different widths; the nave and two central aisles are slightly narrower than the two outermost aisles. At the bottom of the temple one can admire the magnificent grandiosely-proportioned apse which skilfully reunites different architectural themes; it is crowned by a vault featuring highly original characteristics. Around it, a series of richly decorated chapels opens up.

Cathedral, the wooden choir-stalls.

Cathedral, the eagle-shaped lectern
(Vicente Salinas, 1646).

Cathedral, view of the nav

The main façade of the Cathe
dral, commenced in 1418, lead
onto the Plaza del Ayuntamiento.
features three doors respectively
known as the Tower Door or Doc
of Hell (to the left), Door of Pardo
(in the centre), and Door of the La
Judgement or of the Scribes (to th
right). The Door of Pardon wa
thus named on account of the cu
tom of granting indulgences; it
only opened during the visits
Heads of State or the day in whic
the new Cardinal of Toledo tak
possession of the cathedral. It
flanked by the apostles; the ima;
of Christ appears in the mullion
window with two lights. The tab
portrays the appearance of the V
gin imposing the planet on
Ildefonso.

The Watch Door opens onto the Calle de la Chapine-
ría or de la Feria; it dates back to the end of the XIIIth
century and is the oldest of all of the doors. Various
episodes of the New Testament, attributed to Juán
Alemán, are depicted in its pointed arch. The watch
was incorporated in the XVIth century; the present
one, however, dates back to the XVIIIth century. The
iconography on the organ case is by Diego Copín.

The cloister was built at the request of the Portuguese
archbishop Pedro de Tenorio, the city's great patron.
Work was carried out under the direction of Rodrigo
Alonso in 1381. It consists of two floors built according
to a perfectly square plan with five branches that coin-
cide with those of the Cathedral's nave and aisles. The
galleries are each 52 metres long. The quadripartite
vaults are extremely simple and are only interrupted by
the keys of the Archbishop Tenorio's coat-of arms. The
ground floor houses some frescoes alluding to the saints
of Toledo — Eugenio, Casilda and Eladio — attributed
to Bayeu; another two frescoes representing the martyr

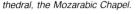

thedral, the Mozarabic Chapel.

Cathedral, Chapel of S. Ildefonso:
the tomb of the Archbishop Albornoz.

thedral, the «Transparent» Monument
*ind the Capilla Mayor.

om of S. Leocadia and S. Daciano are in turn attribut-
to Mariano Maella.

By standing in the nave and turning one's back on the
ain door, one comes face to face with the back part of
e chancel, an excellent example of Gothic art. Exter-
lly this part of the chancel is flanked by three altars
dicated to S. Catalina (to the right), to the Virgin de
Estrella (in the centre) and to Christ (to the left). The
ternal part of the chancel is considered the most beau-
ul in Spain. The lower stalls, built in embossed inlay
Rodrigo Alemán during the XVth century, are deco-
ted with scenes of the conquest of Granada by the
atholic Kings. A series of figures and animals, indicat-
g their author's vivid imagination, are also depicted.
all there are 50 seats in walnut. The upper stalls,
hich are also built in walnut and are clearly in Renais-
nce style, total 70 seats. Alonso de Berruguete is re-
onsible for the choirs to the right; he likewise sculpt-
the Transfiguration in alabaster to be found in the
per part. Those to the right were built by Felipe de
rgoña and can seat 35. Above the archbishop's

throne, one can admire an alabastre frieze once again
representing the investiture of S. Ildefonso, attributed to
Gregorio de Borgoña, Felipe's brother.

The chancel features some invaluable works like the
marble Vergine Blanca dating back to the XIVth century. The bronze spread-eagle pulpit in the centre was
done by Vicente Salinas in 1664. The two organs above
the chancel tribunes are respectively called de la
Epistola (in Baroque style, attributed to Germán López)
and del Evangelio (in Neoclassic style).

The magnificent Capilla Mayor, containing one of the
richest collections of ornaments in Spain, was transformed at the time of Cardinal Cisneros, who had the
royal chapel eliminated to widen the presbytery and
place inside it a large wooden retablo inlaid with gilded, multi-coloured ornaments. Well-known artists like
Copín de Holanda, Enrique Egas, Gumiel, and others
contributed to the creation of this masterpieces.

The retablo narrates scenes from the life of Jesus
Christ and its central part contains an image of the Virgin Mary with Baby Jesus. To the left, one comes across

19

*Cathedral, two views of the
Capitular Hall frescoed
by Jean de Bourgogne.*

*Cathedral, the Santiago Chapel
with the tombs of Alvaro de Luna and
his wife Doña Juana Pimentel;
the XVth century retablo is attributed
to Juan de Segovia, Pedro Gumiel
and Sancho di Zamora.*

Cathedral, the Capilla de los Reyes Nuevos.

Cathedral, the Virgen Blanca in the chancel.

Cathedral, the vault of the Sacristy frescoed by Luca Giordano

the sepulchre of Cardinal Pedro Mendoza with exqui
sitely worked flying angels.

The other side is closed by a XIVth century style
grating. At each end of the retablo are to be found sar
cophagi of the various Castilian kings such as Alfonso
VII, Sancho III and Sancho IV.

The most outstanding of the large windows in this
cathedral is the so-called transparent window, commis
sioned by Cardinal Astorga at the beginning of the
XVIIIth century to let in more light to this part of the
temple. It was built by Narciso Tomé and a predomi
nance of Baroque style is evident not only on accoun

Cathedral, «El Expolio» by El Greco, kept in the Sacristy.

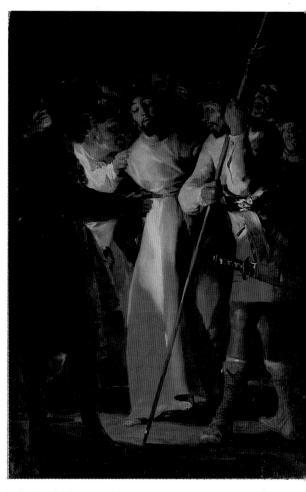

Cathedral, the Capture of Jesus by Goya, hung in the Sacristy.

Cathedral, the «Virgen del Sagrario» patron of the cit

of the profusion of juxtaposed themes, but also due to the use of various materials. This large window lights up the altar of the transparent window, a Baroque work par excellence, carried out once again by Narciso Tomé. In the centre one can admire the Virgen de la Buena Leche or Madonna of Good Milk.

One of the most interesting chapels is the Chapel of S. Ildefonso which houses the sepulchre of Archbishop Albornoz, famous for his battles against Islam. The retablo of the high altar presents the appearance of the Virgin to the Saint yet again. It was achieved by Ventura Rodríguez in veined marble and bronze.

The Chapter-House, also commissioned by Cardinal Cisneros, is a large rectangular room where the Cathedral Chapter used to meet. It is by Pedro Gumiel and Enrique Egas and was completed in 1512. It is worth taking special note of the ceiling of the anteroom in

Moorish or «mujedar» style, an architectural style in vogue in Spain from the XIIIth to the XVIth centuries the portal combined plateresque ornamental elements that are elegantly worked with Moorish decorative pat terns, both in the stucco jambs and architrave. The ceil ing boasts a gold decoration which has remained almos intact.

The Chapel of Santiago was erected by Alvaro de Luna during the XIVth century. It contains his tomb and that of his wife, Juana Pimentel, both in alabastre The Gothic altar is by Juan de Segovia, Sancho de Za mora and Gumiel, and is crowned by a relief represent ing the legend of the apostle Santiago fighting the pa gans during the Battle of Clavijo.

The Chapel of the New Kings is thus named due to the fact that it contains the sepulchres of the three kings of the House of Trastámara: Enrique II, Enrique III and

*Cathedral, the portal
of the Capilla de San Pedro.*

*Cathedral, the aedicula of the Descension
(XVIth century) in the left aisle.*

*Cathedral, Capilla de San Juan:
the rich ostensory attributed to
Enrique de Arfe (XVIth century).*

Juán I with their respective wives. The cenotaphs of the former two portray figures lying down whereas the third cenotaph presents a figure praying. This chapel, which unites numerous styles, has a Gothic structure, but its ornamental elements are decidedly plateresque.

The Sacresty lies to the left of the Capilla Mayor. The visitor's eye is automatically caught by the vault fresco painted by Luca Giordano during the XVIIth century; here, too, the theme of the investiture of S. Ildefonso thanks to the Virgin Mary is repeated. The Virgin is lit up by a ray coming from a central light containing the inscription of Yavhé in Hevrew letters, surrounded by heavenly bodies. Other precious works of art are to be found here, including Van Dyck's «Holy Family» and «St. Inés» and, of major importance, El Greco's works. The most outstanding one is undoubtedly «El Expolio» painted in 1577, which, together with «St. Peter's

Tears» is one of the most moving of all paintings. To the right of the altar, Goya's «Capture of Jesus» is hung. The collection is completed by the series of Apostles, which includes thirteen paintings dedicated to Jesus and to each of the twelve Disciples.

Of the remaining chapels, it is worth mentioning the Chapels of St. Peter and of the Appearance of the Virgin Mary. The former dates back to the XVIIth century; above the external arch, sixteen marble images portray St. Peter, Archbishop Sancho de Rojas and dignitaries of the time. The latter is built on the spot where, according to tradition, the Virgin appeared to the Patron Saint of the temple, a theme repeated several times in the cathedral. The altar in alabastre and bronze was built by Felipe de Borgoña; to the right the stone on which the Virgin Mary placed her feet when she appeared is on display behind a small grating.

ZOCODOVER SQUARE

On leaving the cathedral, continue down Calle Arco del Palacio. Hombre del Palo and del Comercio until you come to Zocodover Square. This irregularly-shaped square has been the hub of Toledo since the Middle Ages. It is a meeting place for foreigners and locals who arrange to meet in the various open air «terrazas» where the best marzipan in Spain is served. In Mohammedan times, the square was the market-place or «zoco» in Arabic; products and articles belonging to the Moorish, Jewish and Christian cultures were exchanged. On the eastern side, one can observe the Arco de la Sangre or Blood Arch, where prisoners were executed at daybreak centuries ago. This door provides access to the Museum of St. Cruz and offers one of the most spectacular views of the city and its hills.

Plaza de Zocodover, overview.

*A charming view
of the cathedral at night.*

*Museo de Santa Cruz
the portal of access*

MUSEUM OF ST. CRUZ

This museum is housed in the homonymous hospital commissioned by Cardinal Mendoza under the direction of Enrique Egas at the beginning of the XVIth century. It is an elegant example of plateresque style. It is built according to a Greek cross plan: the two floors are linked by a beautiful plateresque staircase attributed to Covarrubias; four aisles encompass the three courtyards surrounded by semicircular arcades.

The museum was created to mark the fourth centenary of the death of Charles V and contains works from the XVth, XVIth, XVIIth and XVIIIth centuries; of these works, the most noteworthy belong to the XVI and XVIIth centuries, when Spanish culture flourished. «The Annunciation» «The Assumption» and «Christ

Museo de Santa Cruz:
the Assumption of the Virgin by El Greco.

Museo de Santa Cruz:
the Annunciation by El Greco.

useo di Santa Cruz: two of the original wards
the old homonymous hospital.

useo de Santa Cruz:
e plateresque grand staircase.

agony» are on display in Room 7, together with paintings dedicated to Saints and episodes from their lives. Room 6 features two of José de Ribera's works: «The Sacred Family in Nazareth» and the «Deposition». Furthermore, there are portraits and paintings with military themes such as the one called «Cavalry» (Room 4). Alonso Berruguete's «Visitation Retablo» is to be found in Room 5, whereas «Christ on the cross» is in Room 9. Apart from its collection of paintings, the museum boasts sculptures and precious ornamental elements such as Charles V's bust in bronze (Room 3) and the ivory cross dating back to the XVIIIth century (Room 9). Special mention must be made of the series of tapestries dedicated to the «History of Abraham» of the XVIth century (Room 1), «Los Astrolabios» or signs of the zodiac, worked in the laboratory of Arras (Room 2), sixteen pieces narrating the life of Saint Paul (Room 3) and the series dedicated to Alexander the Great (Room 8).

31

Museo de los Concilios y de la Cultura Visigoda:
view of the interior.

*Casa de Mesa (XVth century) which houses
the Academy of Literature, Sciences and Arts:
one of the interiors.*

MUSEUM OF THE COUNCILS
AND VISIGOTH CULTURE

It would appear that it was originally a Visigoth church which was then converted into a mosque when the city was conquered by the Moors. It was restored at the beginning of the XIIIth century to transform it into a Christian place of worhisp named S. Román. It is built according to a basilican plan with a nave and two aisles and features Caliphal arches in contrast with the Visigoth capitals, the Romanesque «murales» and Renaissance ornamental elements to be found inside the apse.

This museum is full of articles of Visigoth culture and art. Two reproductions of great interest are known as the «Coronas de Guarrazar», bearing witness to the standards achieved by these populations in goldwork, managing to adapt Byzantine techniques to their own conceptions and requirements. The collection includes capitals, fragments of columns and works of art in stone as well as smaller pieces such as personal effects, brooches, diadems and necklaces. «El credo de la Fe», of which only a fragment remains, narrates the conversion of King Recaredo to Catholicism.

33

House and Museum of El Greco: the outside of the building.

El Greco's house: the patio.

El Greco's house: the artist's studio with his «St. Peter Penitent» in the centre.

El Greco's house: the kitchen.

THE HOUSE AND MUSEUM OF EL GRECO

The architectural lines of El Greco's house are typical of Toledo and characteristic of the city's most cosmopolitan period. It is a two storey building and almost all the rooms overlook a central courtyard. It does not only contain the artist's household goods but also important paintings. In one of the rooms on the top floor, «St. Peter Penitent» is on display supported by an easel while the Flemish painting known as «The Summer» is hung on the wall. The paintings of «St. Francis and his Brother Lion» are to be

*El Greco's house: «San Bernardino»
painted by El Greco in 1603 at the
altar of the homonymous chapel.*

*The mudéjar bell-tower
of the Church of Santo Tomé.*

found in the adjoining room. On the top floor of the museum next to the house, one can admire a painting portraying the Saint alongside three mitres, a symbol of the episcopal dignity that he was offered on three occasions and which he refused each time. One can catch a glimpse of the Moorish tower of the Church of Saint Tomé from the house's garden.

CHURCH OF ST. TOME

The existing temple was built by Count de Orgaz at his own expense on the site of an old mosque. His generosity and his numerous other virtues gave rise to a legend that describes the miracle which occurred at the time of his death when St. Sebastian and St. Augustine descended from heaven for his burial. This moment has been immortalized in the painting which has been kept in this church since its completion. The complexity of composition justifies a great simplicity in the treatment of colours and shapes in «El Entierro del Conde de Orgaz» which is considered El Greco's masterpiece a

Church of Santo Tomé: The Burial of the Count de Orgaz (El Greco, 1584).

Museum of Taller del Moro: view of the interior.

well as one of the greatest works of art in the world. The scene is divided into two parts by a horizontal line of horsemen of that period, one of whom represents a self-portrait of the artist. In the upper part, one can observe Jesus surrounded by heavenly bodies on receiving the Count's soul, which is suggested by a translucid shape. As in the representation of the panorama of Toledo, here too the artist's son is in the foreground and with his faraway look, he seems to be inviting us to enter an extraterritorial world.

MUSEUM OF THE «TALLER DEL MORO»

This laboratory was annexed to the cathedral; the various pieces of stone which were then placed as ornaments in various parts of the temple were worked here. It contains some magnificent plaster inlay work in pure Moorish style, as well as some ceramics and tile or «azulejos» works which are very typical of that period.

Synagogue of the Tránsito: the interior and one of the rooms of the Museo Sefardí.

Church of San Juan de los Reyes: the left side.

THE TRANSIT SYNAGOGUE

Patronized by Samuel Levi, a rich Jew who was the treasurer and personal friend of Pedro the Cruel, this richly decorated synagogue in Moorish style dates back to the mid-XIVth century. In the upper part, over fifty arches are supported by coupled grey and pink columns; some of these arches frame windows. The main part features three alcoves separated by columns that support multifoiled arches where the Holy Scriptures are kept. The friezes include scriptures in Hebrew letters. On the right wall, one can observe the women's galleries where the women attended religious services. At present this synagogue houses the Sephardi Museum in an annex.

S. JUAN DE LOS REYES

Commissioned by the Catholic Kings, this extraordinary monastery of the «Isabellian» Gothic period dates back to the last quarter of the XVth century; it commemorates the victory of the Catholic Kings over the roups of Alfonso V of Portugal during the Battle of Toro.

Juan Guas was entrusted with the work, but the north portal was placed in the hands of Covarrubias.

From this portal hung a series of chains used by the Moors when emprisoning Christians, later freed with the reconquest of Granada; these chains were brought here by Ferdinand and Isabelle as a symbol of the final defeat of the pagans. Napoleon's troops set fire to the monastery in 1808 and amongst other things, both the chains as well as the panes of glass covering the temple's large windows were destroyed. The church, with its simple, harmonious lines, features some interesting columns that branch out from the capital, forming a series of ribbings in the vaults of the nave and the aisles. Ferdinand and Isabelle's coat-of-arms is repeated several times as an ornamental pattern.

According to popular opinion, the cloister is the leading «Isabellian» Gothic building. It consists of two floors linked by a platersque staircase, attributed to Covarrubias. The stone patterns are the outstanding ornamental elements of the downstairs part of the cloister, blending in beautifully with the structures of the vaults, the countless figures of animals and monsters and with a series of images of saints, without ever losing the balance and sobriety that have made this cloister so famous. The upper floor is oustanding on account of the elegance of the shapes and the proportions of the volumes. Here one can admire some arches crowned by stone lions supporting the coats-of-arms of the kindgoms united by Ferdinand and Isabelle.

41

Church of San Juan de los Reyes:
view of the interior.

Church of San Juan de los Reyes: from top to
bottom and from left to right:
the exterior of the apse, the portico of the cloister,
a partial view of the cloister seen
from above the another view
of the open gallery of the cloister.

Synagogue of Santa María la Blanca:
view of the interior (in the apse, XVth century retablo)
and detail of the horse-shoe shaped arches.

The House-Museum of Victorio Macho

The old Bridge de San Martín
dating back to the XIIIth century

SYNAGOGUE OF S. MARIA LA BLANCA

This synagogue, which most probably dates back to the XIIth century with reconstructions during the following century, is one of Toledo's oldest monuments. During the course of its history, it was used not only for worship but also for military purposes and even as a warehouse. It was restored once and for all in 1851 and as a result has reacquired its former glory. Thirty-two octagonal columns support iron arches, forming a nave and four aisles. The capitals are an elegant piece of Moorish plaster cast; each has its own distinctive features but blends in perfectly with the others as there is a certain homogeneity of style. Each aisle contains a chapel in plateresque style, all skillfully integrated in the context of the general Arab style. The dome of the central chapel rests on four pendentives which feature gilded shells conjoined by others, which are also gilded among the fluting of the wood.

On leaving through the garden and bearing right, ne comes across the Museum of Victorio Macho, a ontemporary sculptor who settled in Toledo in 1952. he museum houses some of his works, the most fa- ous of which are the statues of his mother and broth- ; they both reveal balance of proportions and mastery technique.

'HE BRIDGE OF S. MARTIN

It was built during the XIIIth century and restored uring the following century thanks to Archbishop :norio because it had been damaged during the battles ught by Pedro I, the Cruel, against his brother nrique de Trastámara. During the siege of 1368, the :sieged deliberately destroyed the central arch to pre- :nt the city from being taken by the invaders. The one bridge consists of five arches and features a de- nce tower at each end. The one that faces the city

presents on the one side a relief in granite dedicated to the Virgin of the Tabernacle and, on the other, the shield with the city's coats-of-arms.

THE WALLS

Toledo has always been fortified, especially to the north, as it is the only side unprotected by the depres- sion that forces the Tagus to form a natural bend around almost the entire rise on which the city stands. The Romans built a defence system that extended from the praetorium, which is now the Alcazar, to St. Tomé, touching Zocodover, to once again reach the existing Alcazar. The Visigoth walls were longer: they started from the existing Alcazar, extended as far as Santa Cruz, touching the Puerta de los Doce Cantos, the Puerta del Cambrón, the Transit gardens and S. Sebastiano to return once again to the Puerta de los Doce Cantos. These walls were damaged several times during the war aginst the Moors, who then had to re- store them.

47

he Gate of the Cambrón
ith Toledo's coat of arms.

Hospital de Tavera: overview.

LA PUERTA DEL CAMBRON

This Renaissance style gate was built in 1576 to re-place the previous one which was built by the Visigoth king Wamba. The façade facing the city is characterized by a statue of S. Leocadia attributed to Berruguete. The other façade bears the shield with the coat-of-arms of Toledo. There are slate-roofed towers at both sides and fragments of Roman and Arab buildings are incorporated in the tower itself.

TAVERA HOSPITAL

This hospital was founded in 1541 by Juan Pardo de Tavera, Archbishop of Toledo and General Inquisitor. It is situated in front of the Gate of Bisagra, which is why it is also known as the «Hospital de Afuera». The works ended in 1603 and famous architects contributed to its construction, from Bustamante to Covarrubias and from González de Lara to Vergara. The outside walls were completed during the XVIIIth century. The style is Renaissance with echoes of Florentine palaces. The three-storey façade is built of granite.

The courtyard is divided by a corridor which crosses it from the entrance to the church dedicated to St. John the Baptist, whose door in Carrara marble is attributed to Berruguete. It consists of only a nave; the plan is a Roman cross, in the centre of which is the tomb of the cardinal who founded the building, also attributed to Berruguete. In the underground crypts, members of the families of the Dukes of Lerma and Medinaceli are buried.

The west wing of the hospital was transformed into a palace by the Duke of Lerma during the XVIIth century and into a museum in 1940 by the homonymous foundation. This palace is the emblem of all the splendour of the high society of that era and contains valuable works pertaining to its museological collection and which are distributed among its various rooms. In the dining-hall, one can admire an equestrian portrait of the Emperor Charles V, painted by Sánchez Coello, as well as other paintings of nobles of that period. The Archives not only house all the documents relating to the building of the hospital but also exhibit «The Holy Family» by El Greco, not to mention «The Philosopher» and the discussed «La Mujer Barbuda» or «Bearded Woman», both by Ribera. In the room called Greco one can admire the portrait of Cardinal Tavera, built according to the model of the prelate's death-mask, «St. Peter's Tears» and «St. Francis»; it is most definitely worth tak-

Hospital de Tavera: the patio.

Hospital de Tavera: Museum of the Duchess of
Lerma: the Holy Family by El Greco.

Hospital de Tavera, Museum of the Duchess of Lerm
the Archives and the Duchess's bedroor

ing a look at «Christ's Baptism» on account of th
magnificence of the unusual colours and dimensions. E
Greco's works are displayed alongside portraits of aris
tocrats of that period painted by Zurbarán an
Bartolomé González and two tapestries of the XVIt
and XVIIth centuries. The duchess's bedrooms house
various paintings: Tintoretto's «Holy Family», tw
works by Luca Giordano — «St. Gregory's Mass» an
«The Prayer in the Vegetable Garden» — and anothe
painting from the Italian school, «Jesus, Martha an
Mary», together with a Gothic crucifix above th
bedhead. The duke's room contains a portrait of the las
descendant of the Lermas, painted by Sotomayor, an
another portrait of the mother, the Duchess o
Medinaceli, achieved by Edouard Dubufé in 1861. A
point of interest in this room is created by the sma
painting of the Flemish school depicting a shipwrec
caused by demons. Of the furniture, it is worth notin
the ebony and ivory cabinet portraying various scene
from the bible. Lastly, in the chapel's vestibule, one ca
admire a painting by Snyders with hunting scenes. It i
also interesting to visit the pharmacy dating back to th
XVIIth century where period instruments are kept.

THE NEW GATE OF BISAGRA

This is the city's most famou
gate and the one encountere
when coming from Madrid; it date
back to 1550. To the sides of th
tower itself and on the outside ar
two imposing towers equipped wit
loopholes for defence purposes tha
almost reach ground level. On th
gate one can admire an enormou
frieze in granite portraying a two
headed eagle. Above they built
pediment crowned by an ange
who keeps guard over the cit
brandishing a sword. The façad
facing the city one again bears th
coat-of-arms of Toledo and to th
sides it features two square tower
crowned with two pyramida
domes covered with green an
white tiles. It is the work of th
maestro Covarrubias. According t
some authors the name of this gat

*The Cristo de la Vega kept in the Church
of S. Leocadia, built on the
site of a Visigoth basilica.*

The strong Puerta Nueva de Bisagra.

Two pictures of the Puerta Vieja de Bisagra, also known as the Gate of Alfonso VI.

could come from *via sacra*, with the inhabitants of Toledo emulating the homonymous street in Rome. Another theory maintains that the name is originally Arab: «bab» meaning gate and «shara» meaning red; what gave rise to this theory is the presence of red clays towards the north of the city.

THE OLD GATE OF BISAGRA OR OF ALFONSO VI

It is generally believed that this gate was built at the beginning of the IXth century. Arab art is present in the lower part and Moorish architecture in the upper part. Tradition has it that that Alfonso VI entered through this gate after his troops had reconquered the city on the 25th May 1085.

Church of Santiago de Arrabal: the exterior.

Church of Santiago de Arrabal: the interior.

THE CHURCH OF SANTIAGO DE ARRABAL

It would appear that this temple was built on the site where a mosque originally stood. As in the case of many other churches in Toledo, this church was commissioned by Alfonso VI. A peculiarity of this church is its bell-tower completely detached from the rest of the building, which is an uncommon sight in Spain. It consists of a nave and two aisles where stone and decorative brick alternate, creating an appearance of placid sobriety. It is worth noting the XIVth century pulpit in the left aisle, which is famous because it was where S. Vicente Ferrer delivered his fervent sermons thanks to which he managed to convert numerous Jews to the Roman faith. The restored work of the high altar portrays the apostle Santiago in the centre.

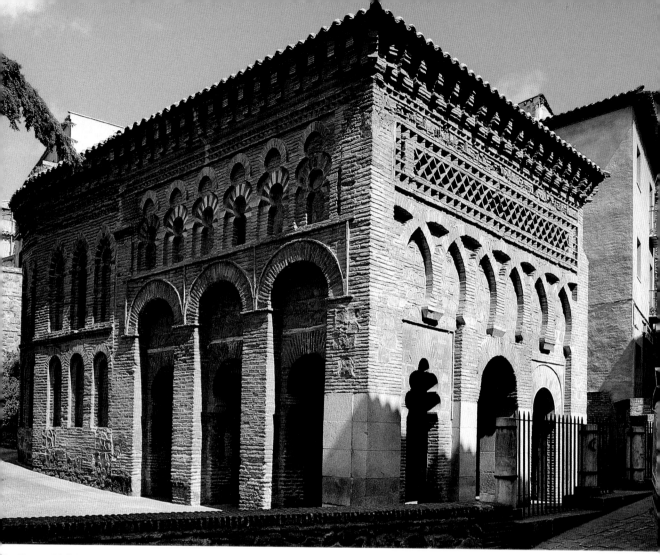

The Puerta del Sol.

The Church of Cristo de la Luz.
already a mosque

LA PUERTA DEL SOL

This Moorish gate is to be found near the Gate of Bisagra at the end of the Calle Real del Arrabal and in the direction of Zocodover Square. Like many other typical buildings in Toledo, it is built in stone and brick. It was constructed at the time of Archbishop Tenorio and it is presumed that it was used as the main entrance to the city. It consists of two fortified towers which differ one from the other as the left one is round while the right one is square. The central body is in stone, whereas the ornamental battlements are in brick. Two stone columns support the main pointed arch.

The marble shield above the access arch one again represents the Virgin Mary imposing the planet on S. Ildefonso. In the upper part of the shield the sun and moon are portrayed, indicating the city's interest in astronomy and science, possibly giving rise to the name of the gate itself. An unusual iconograph is to be found in the centre: two women holding a tray on which a man's head rests. It is generally believed that the head belonged to a certain Fernando González, a town officer, who used violence against two young women; Ferdinand III the Saint therefore obtained his beheadal and insisted that the scene be immortalized in stone to act as a public warning.

THE MOSQUE OF CRISTO DE LA LUZ

Originally this temple was probably a place of prayer and worship for the Visigoths; it is thought to have been founded by Atanagildo. It was transformed and converted into a mosque by the invading Moors and then trans-

he Church of Cristo de la Luz: the typical orse-shoe shaped arches of the interior.

The dome with Spanish-Moorish decorations dating back to the XVth century of the church of the Convento de la Concepcion.

ormed into a Christian church once again after the econquest of Toledo by Alfonso VI, who had a mass fficiated here as thanksgiving for his victory over the agans.

The three arches of the doors of the internal façade re all different and are accompanied by a series of in-rtwined arches. An Arab engraving reads: ONLY ALLAH IS GREAT. Indoors two areas can be distinguished. The first, at the entrance, is a square with a series of columns crowned by domes, which are all different and which rest on walls and pillars, four of which have Visigoth capitals. The second part is in Moorish style and contains frescoes of the XIIIth century in a precarious state of repair.

*A picture of the Castle of San Servando,
at the foot of which stands
the Alcántara bridge.*

THE CASTLE OF S. SERVANDO

This castle stands on a hill in front of the Alcántara bridge. On this site stood a fortification built in Roman times; the oldest parts of the existing building were, however, erected by the Moors. It was completely restored by Alfonso VI after the reconquest of the city and was always used as a bulwark for the defence of the left side of the river. Some sources maintain that El Cid Campeador was appointed governor of the castle; it was then handed over to the Knight Templars. Other sourc-

es support the theory that Alfonso VI built it and gav it to the Cluny monks whose convent was in the vicinit of the castle. It was abandoned during the XIIth centur as a result of repeated attacks by the Moors. It was seri ously damaged during the war between Pedro the Crue and his brother Enrique de Trastámara. In 1945 th castle was handed over to the «Delegación d Juventudes», who restored it and converted it into school.

San Juan de Dios, a typical alley in Toledo.

THE STREETS OF TOLEDO

Walking along the streets of Toledo means walking through Visigoth, Mohammedan and Jewish Spain. The vast majority of these streets stand out on account of their curves, narrowness and abundance of monuments. Toledo has changed very little over the past four centuries managing to preserve its churches, houses, walls and buildings. Some streets narrow all of a sudden and sometimes are linked to others through flights of steps; this blocks traffic but facilitates tourists sparing them long walks in search of places of historic and artistic interest. Often the names of the streets bear witness to past traditions and legends, activities and customs.

The name of the Calle de los Alfileritos, for example, comes from an old custom. At number 24 one can observe an alcove with a statue of the Virgin Mary in front of which the young maidens to be married used to press their large, coloured hairpins into their hair having pricked themselves slightly in the hopes of obtaining the Virgin Mary's protection in their search for the husband of their dreams. Legend has it that this custom dates back to the XVIth century, when a noble lady, separated from her loved one as he had gone to war with Charles V, prayed to the Virgin Mary day and night for the return of her knight. When she could no longer keep awake, her lady-in-waiting, had orders to prick her with one of her pins which at daybreak was offered to the Virgin Mary as a sign of the sacrifice of numerous nightwatches. After many years of hopeful waiting, the knight returned safe and sound, giving credit to the belief that this Virgin Mary listened to the prayers of the young sweethearts.

The Calle del Hombre del Palo or «street of the man with the wooden stick» is thus named because one day an engineer, none other than Charles V's watchmaker — Juanelo Turriano — presented in public a wooden machine with human features and made it walk along this very road.

Some of the best local handicrafts shops line Calle de San Juan de Dios. These shops usually exhibit their merchandise on the outside walls of their houses.

*Some significant examples of local
handicraft production: pottery and swords.*

HANDICRAFTS IN TOLEDO

Local handicrafts can be roughly divided into four main activities that occupy the vast majority of the local population: ceramics, sword manufacture, damascening and the production of Toledo's most typical sweet: marzipan. Toledo's swords and daggers are world famous. For example, every year at the Academia General Militar del Cile the best cadet officer is ceremoniously awarded a sabre manufactured here by the Head of State. Having visited the city and appreciated the ele-

gance and skill with which these swords are manufactured, tourists often yield to temptation and buy one as a souvenir of their stay in Toledo.

These swords are handmade according to procedures and techniques that have been handed down from father to son for countless generations. They start off as nothing more than a piece of steel, which is then forged, hardened, hammered and flattened until the required thickness is obtained. They are then cooled in

large water containers before being smoked for a matter of minutes to obtain that typical blue-grey colour; in this way one obtains the blade to which the hilt is then welded. At this stage, all that remains to be done is to is impress the colours with special paints, a task that requires extreme dexterity because of the attention required in impressing even the most minute details.

From some points of view, damascening is very similar to sword manufacture: a steel blade is encrusted with gold filigree and then treated with special enamels to obtain diversified, elegant patterns on a wide range of objects.

Today's ceramic industry owes its abundance of themes and technical skill to the fusion of elements of the three cultures that meet here. The result of this artistic integration is what is currently known as Moorish style which, combining precision and dexterity in the use of colour, gives rise to highly decorative architectural elements and ornamental household goods.

The marzipan is prepared with almonds and sugar. Toledo's industries stand out because of their refined elegant wrappings. The word «mazapán» probably comes from the Arab custom to preserve sweets and spices in special boxes called *mahasaban* in Arabic.

CONTENTS